DATE DUE			

Best Jokes & Riddles

Compiled by Anna Pansini
Illustrated by Carolyn Loh

Troll Associates

A TROLL BOOK, published by Troll Associates,
Mahwah, NJ 07430

Printed in the United States of America.
10 9 8 7 6 5 4 3 2 1

What Makes You Laugh?

When we asked kids across America to send in their favorite jokes for Troll's **Great Giggle and Riddle Contest,** the response was incredible! Riddles, knock-knock jokes, funny lines about monsters, animals, and ghosts—thousands of zany jokes from kids came pouring in.

The result of the contest is two terrific books—this one, and a companion book called *Great Riddles, Giggles & Jokes.* They're each filled with 350 of *your* best jokes.

The contestant's name appears under each joke. (When we received duplicate jokes, we chose the earliest entry.) Both books contain an alphabetical listing of winners, along with their age or grade, school, and school address.

Finally, we'd like to thank all the children who entered the contest, and the teachers who encouraged them.

Classroom Capers

Teacher: Tim, what did you write your report on?
Tim: A piece of paper.

James Sunny

Father: What did you learn in school today?
Daughter: My teacher taught us writing.
Father: What did you write?
Daughter: I don't know. She hasn't taught us reading yet.

Cindy Garrison

Teacher: Who can tell me where the English Channel is?
Jane: I don't know. It's not on my TV.

Lorena S. Pecson

Why do teachers take aspirin?
For de-tension headaches.

Andy Symonds

Student: Teacher, I can't do this problem.
Teacher: Any six-year-old should be able to do it.
Student: Well, no wonder I can't. I'm ten.

Lisa Frohnheiser

Teacher: Bobby, if I have two sandwiches and you have two sandwiches, what do we have?
Bobby: LUNCH!

Anthony Santoli

Teacher: What is your favorite state, Sam?
Sam: Mississippi.
Teacher: How do you spell it?
Sam: Er... I like Ohio much better.

Katie Callan

First Person: How did you do on your history exam?
Second Person: Not very well, but it wasn't my fault. They asked me about things that happened before I was born.

Jonas Young

Teacher: What's the chemical formula for water?
Student: H, i, j, k, l, m, n, o.
Teacher: May I ask what that is?
Student: That's what you said last week, "Water is H to O."

Aaron Mangabang

Principal: Young man, I have to say you're different from the rest of the students.
Student: Really!
Principal: Yes, they're graduating.

Tommy Arbour

George: There was a riot in the library.
Kyle: What happened?
George: Somebody found "dynamite" in the dictionary.

Joshua M. Sheehan

Teacher: Why are you writing that letter so slowly?
Student: Because it's to my sister, and she can't read fast.

Joy Fike

Mother: What did you learn in school today?
Daughter: How to talk without moving my lips.

Holly Kobolt

Phil: Jack, what smells in the lunchroom?
Jack: I don't know.
Phil: Your nose!

April Gobel

First Student: Were the test questions easy?
Second Student: The questions were easy. The answers were hard.

AnnMarie Podobinski

Teacher: How did you get that horrible swelling on your nose?
Scott: I bent over to smell a brose.
Teacher: There's no B in rose.
Scott: There was in this one.

Jessica Schmelzer

Teacher: Put the words "detail," "defeat" and "defense" in a sentence.
Student: I already have mine.
Teacher: Okay, read it.
Student: Defeat of de fox went over defense before detail.

Amy Heineke

Teacher: Why do we sometimes call the Middle Ages the Dark Ages?
Polly: Because there were so many knights.

Taylor Strait

It's Raining Riddles

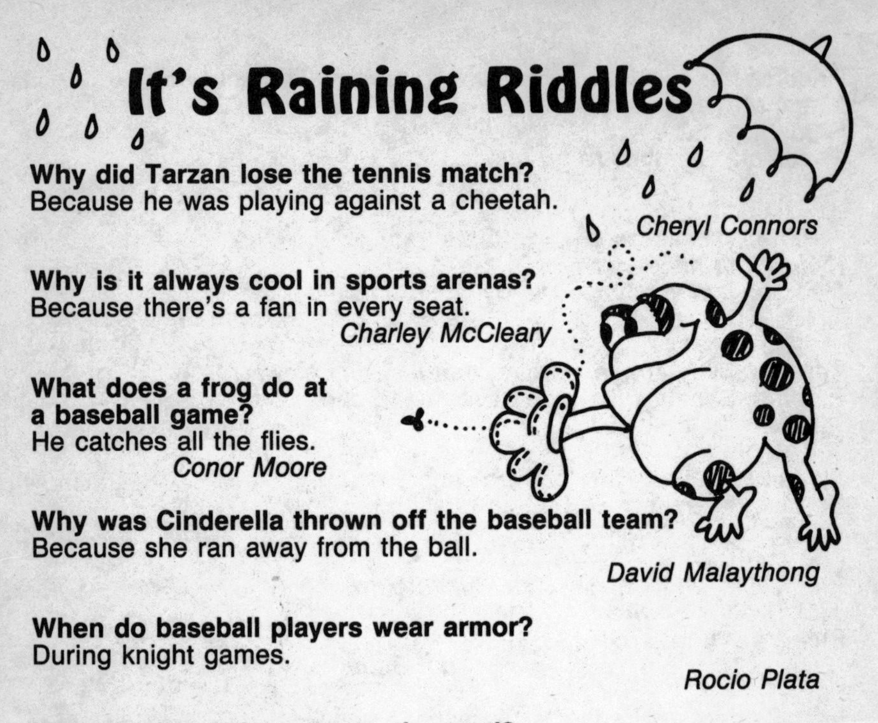

Why did Tarzan lose the tennis match?
Because he was playing against a cheetah.

Cheryl Connors

Why is it always cool in sports arenas?
Because there's a fan in every seat.

Charley McCleary

What does a frog do at a baseball game?
He catches all the flies.

Conor Moore

Why was Cinderella thrown off the baseball team?
Because she ran away from the ball.

David Malaythong

When do baseball players wear armor?
During knight games.

Rocio Plata

Why did the skeleton cross the road?
To get to the body shop.

Matt Enderby

Who plays when he works, and works hard when he plays?
A one-man band.

Stefanie Stombres

Why is it a bad idea to do math problems in the jungle?
Because if you add 4 + 4, you get ate (8).

Laura Friese

What weighs almost nothing, but can't be held for long?
Your breath.

Jimmy Cunat

What comes once in a minute, twice in a moment, and never in a thousand years?
The letter M.

Liam E. Harrison

What has 12 tails, one horn, and squeals?
A dozen pigs in a livestock truck.

Vanessa Galati

If you had 10 pounds of feathers and 10 pounds of bricks, which would weigh more?
Neither, they both weigh the same.

Libby Wasilchuk

It's a dark, freezing cold night. You have been wandering in a blizzard for a day and a half. You spot a log cabin. You go in it and see a wood-burning stove, a kerosene lamp, an oil burner, and one candle. You only have one match. What do you light first?
The match.

John Smythe

What is worse than a giraffe with a sore throat?
A centipede with sore feet.

David Reding

What has teeth but doesn't bite?
A comb.

Travis Lee

What has four legs and flies?
A picnic table.

Allison Madonna

What has many leaves but no branches?
A book.

Tommie Denlinger

What word becomes shorter when you add two letters to it?
Short. Add *"er"* and it becomes shorter.

Nicholas Santone

Why is it useless to send a letter to Washington?
Because he died in 1799.

Brenda Lieb

Nutty Knock-Knocks

Knock! Knock!
Who's there?
Horn.
Horn who?
Horn go beep, beep; car go varoom!

Chris Brown

Knock! Knock!
Who's there?
Harry.
Harry who?
Harry up and let me in.

Andrew Fraerman

Knock! Knock!
Who's there?
Alma.
Alma who?
Alma cookies are gone and I want more.

Andrea Arrigo

Knock! Knock!
Who's there?
Orange.
Orange who?
Orange you gonna come and open the door?

Jessica Molinares

Knock! Knock!
Who's there?
Dishes.
Dishes who?
Dishes your friend, open the door.

Denece Hall

Knock! Knock!
Who's there?
Oswald.
Oswald who?
Oswald my bubble gum.

Jodi Furnival

Knock! Knock!
Who's there?
Bear.
Bear who?
Bear with me. I forgot the rest of the joke.
Tabitha Sadowski

Knock! Knock!
Who's there?
Justin.
Justin who?
Justin time for dinner.
Jason Shelton

Knock! Knock!
Who's there?
Dwayne.
Dwayne who?
Dwayne the bathtub, I'm drowning.
Stephanie DeLano

Help!

Knock! Knock!
Who's there?
Ben.
Ben who?
Ben looking all over for you.
Danny Nieken

Knock! Knock!
Who's there?
Jaws.
Jaws who?
Jaws truly.
Matt McClendon

Knock! Knock!
Who's there?
Arthur.
Arthur who?
Arthur any more cookies in the cookie jar?
Haley Dean Tycer

Knock! Knock!
Who's there?
Diploma.
Diploma who?
Diploma has come to fix your faucet.
Robert Hines

Riddle Dee-Dee

What's green and white and goes 125 miles an hour?
A frog in a white racing car.

Jeremy Barb

When is a piece of string like a piece of wood?
When it has knots in it.

Nikki Evanush

What is just as big as you but doesn't weigh a single pound?
Your shadow.

Cindy Wilson

Why is a bride unlucky on her wedding day?
Because she's not marrying the best man.

Nichole DeLaire

Two men stand at the same fork in the road. One man always lies and the other man always tells the truth, but you don't know which man is which. They can talk to each other, but you can only talk to one of the men. What question will you ask, and which man should you ask it of in order to find out the correct road to follow?
You can ask either man, "Which way will the other man tell me to go?" You should then go the opposite way because the honest man will tell you what road the liar would tell you to take, which would not be the correct way; and the liar would tell you what road the honest man would not tell you to take, which would not be the correct road.

April Bree Bullock

I can make words disappear and the more you use me, the smaller I become. What am I?
An eraser.

Erica Dattilio

Did you hear the joke about the bed?
It hasn't been made up yet.

Donald Moyer

Why did the chicken cross the park?
To get to the other slide.

David Bonarigo

What's black and white and red all over?
A zebra with the measles.

Eric Day

Space Solos

How does the man in the moon cut his hair?
Eclipse it!

Steven Ciregna

When is the moon going broke?
When it's down to its last quarter.
Marlena Russell

How do Martians shave?
With laser blades.

Mike Butala

Did you hear about the new restaurant on the moon?
Great food, but no atmosphere.
Lucilla Dagostino

What was the first animal in space?
The cow. It jumped over the moon.
Jessicah Gallagher

A very far-out looking alien from Mars went to the doctor. After the examination the doctor said, "I'm very sorry but you have heart trouble." The alien replied, "I want a second opinion." The doctor said, "Okay. You're ugly too."

Rebecca Bledsoe

What do you do to get ready for an astronaut's birthday party?
You plan-et.

Brian Pruitt

Sue: Did you know the astronauts found some bones on the moon?
Betty: Oh, dear! I guess the cow didn't make it over after all.
Shane Siewert

Which planet is like a circus?
Saturn, because it has 3 rings.

Megan Lantz

Once there was an alien that came from outer space. He landed on Earth near a baby chick. He asked the chick, "Is there a hotel around here?" The chick said, "Cheep! Cheep!" "I hope it is," said the alien. "Getting here cost me a fortune."
Sarah Lloyd

In the Mood for Food

How do you pay compliments to bread?
You toast it.

Emily Baldwin

What is a cheerleader's favorite soft drink?
Root beer.

Stacey Rivenburg

What can't you have for breakfast?
Lunch and dinner.

Sara Minster

Why are bananas so popular?
Because they have a-peel.

Christine Bowen

Why is honey scarce in Boston?
Because there's only one B in Boston.

Jesse Hallowell

Why did the tomato blush?
Because it saw the salad dressing.

Rachna Chandiramani

What do computers eat for a snack?
Micro chips.

Theresa Link

Why did the potato go to France?
Because it wanted to be a French fry.

Lauren Esposito

What kind of shoes do you make out of banana skins?
Slippers.

Stacie Caris

Why did the raisin ask the fig out?
Because he couldn't find a date.

Michael Rivera

How does a hungry man eat a hot dog?
With relish.

Daniel Wright

Where was the first French fry made?
In Greece.

Robert Winkel

Why aren't lemons allowed to sing or play music?
Because they hit too many sour notes.

Jennifer Sprouse

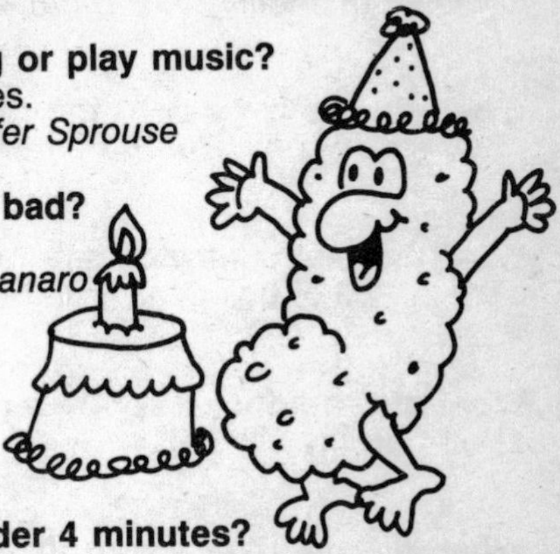

How do you keep milk from going bad?
Leave it in the cow.

Jenny Campanaro

If a pickle is one year old, what should you do?
Wish it "Happy Birthday."

Joleen Tolman

Can a hamburger run a mile in under 4 minutes?
Yes, because it's fast food.

Danny Hushagen

Who leads the popcorn?
The kernel.

Penny Frederickson

What kind of meat do you get from a cow with 2 short legs and 2 long legs?
Lean meat.

Elisha Winston

What is the best thing to put into a pie?
Your teeth.

Kimberly Stewert

What happens when a banana sees a ghost?
The banana splits.

Judy Wang

How do you make a strawberry shake?
Take it to a horror movie.

Cindy Hunter

Which fruits are never lonely?
Bananas and grapes because they hang around in bunches.

Thomas Richard Puffer

Did You Hear That?

What did one elevator say to the other elevator?
"I think I'm coming down with something."

Tonetta Norman

What did the hat say to the coat hanger?
"You stay here while I go on a head."

Thomas Smith

What did one sandwich say to the other sandwich?
"You're full of bologna."

Dan Muskie

What did the duck say when it went shopping?
"Put it on my bill."

Jennifer Tucci

What did one rose say to the other?
"Hi, bud."

Josh Sloan

What did the digital watch say to the grandmother clock?
"Look, Ma! No hands!"

Amanda Church

What do birds say on Halloween?
"Trick or tweet?"

Rebecca Scheffy

What did the porcupine say to the cactus?
"Is that you, Mama?"

Jonathan Kendrick

What do frogs say on the first day of January?
"Have a Hoppy New Year!"

Derron Jones

What did the banana say to the dog?
Nothing, bananas can't talk.

Ryan Horvath

What did the candle say to the other candle?
"Don't birthdays burn you up?"

Kathryn Wood

What did the math book say to the reading book?
"I bet I have more problems than you."

Raquelle Bainter

What did the cowboy say when he landed on a cactus?
"Ouch!"

Joseph Molesky

What did the Pink Panther say when he stepped on an ant?
"Dead ant, dead ant, dead ant, dead ant, dead ant, dead ant."

Marquist Harris

What did the mother rope say to the baby rope?
"Don't be knotty."

Matt Tindall

What did one book say to the other book?
"Where are you bound?"

Angie Taylor

What did the truck driver say when he lost his tire?
"You picked a fine time to leave me loose wheel."

Gary Powers

What did Benjamin Franklin say when he discovered electricity?
Nothing. He was too shocked.

Erin McCracken

What did one wall say to the other wall?
"I'll meet you at the corner."

Andrea Charles

What did the rug say to the floor?
"I've got you covered."

Jason Wootton

What did one penny say to the other penny?
"Let's get together and make some cents."

Anna Moser

How Are You Feeling?

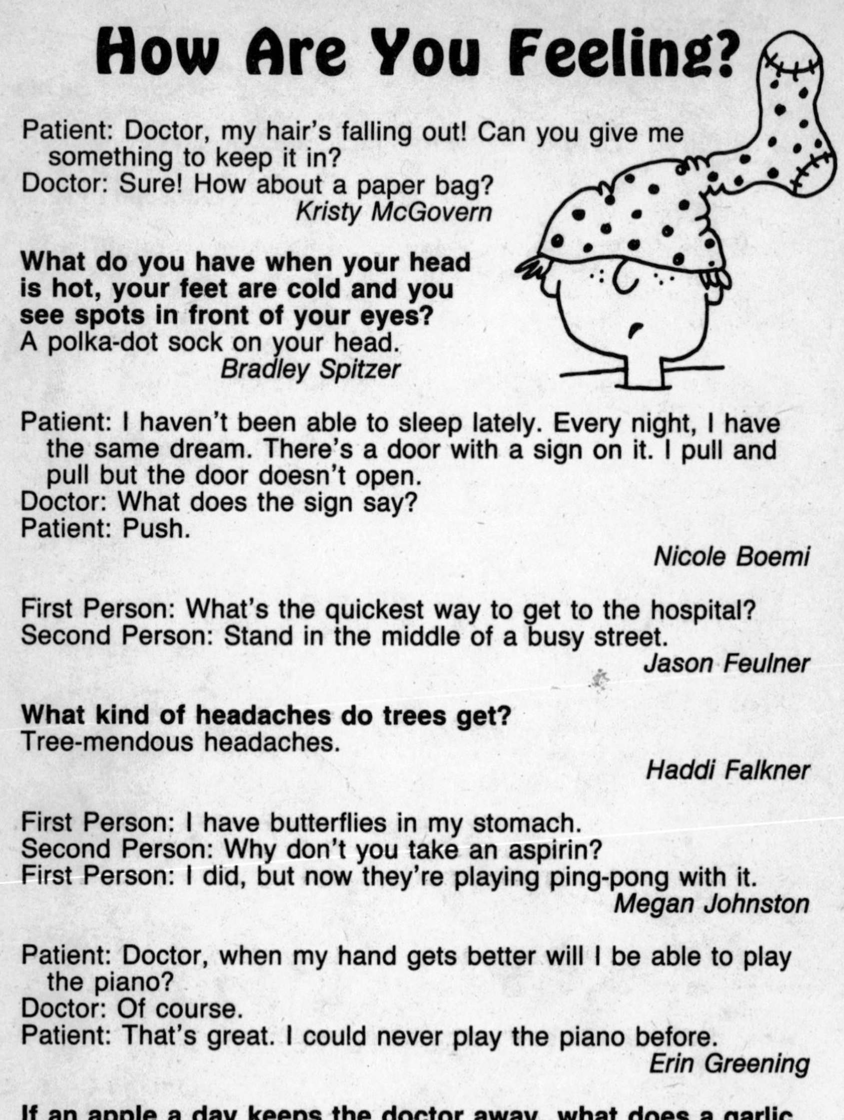

Patient: Doctor, my hair's falling out! Can you give me something to keep it in?
Doctor: Sure! How about a paper bag?
Kristy McGovern

What do you have when your head is hot, your feet are cold and you see spots in front of your eyes?
A polka-dot sock on your head.
Bradley Spitzer

Patient: I haven't been able to sleep lately. Every night, I have the same dream. There's a door with a sign on it. I pull and pull but the door doesn't open.
Doctor: What does the sign say?
Patient: Push.
Nicole Boemi

First Person: What's the quickest way to get to the hospital?
Second Person: Stand in the middle of a busy street.
Jason Feulner

What kind of headaches do trees get?
Tree-mendous headaches.
Haddi Falkner

First Person: I have butterflies in my stomach.
Second Person: Why don't you take an aspirin?
First Person: I did, but now they're playing ping-pong with it.
Megan Johnston

Patient: Doctor, when my hand gets better will I be able to play the piano?
Doctor: Of course.
Patient: That's great. I could never play the piano before.
Erin Greening

If an apple a day keeps the doctor away, what does a garlic clove do?
It keeps everyone away.
Jennifer Mertz

Where do sick boats go?
To the dock.
Christine McCulken

Patient: Doctor, I feel like a deck of cards.
Doctor: I'll deal with you later.
Tara Campbell

Why did the house call the doctor?
Because it had a window pain.
Kevin Twomey

What kind of water should you drink when you are sick?
Well water.
Carmen Beier

Patient: Doctor, I think I'm a bullfrog.
Doctor: How long have you thought this?
Patient: Ever since I was a tadpole.
Jason van der Linde

What should you do when a health specialist knocks at your door?
Vit'am-in.
Kristen McAuliffe

Why did the boy take his comb to the dentist?
Because it lost a tooth.
Brandi Wyatt

Why was the patient laughing after surgery?
Because the doctor left him in stitches.
Patrick Murphy

What did the doctor prescribe to get rid of the measles?
Spot remover.
Amanda Cumberland

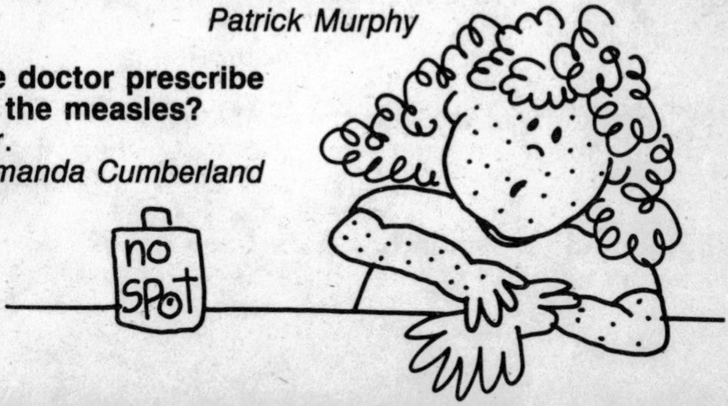

Amusing Animals

What should you do when a bull charges you?
Pay him.

Matthew Williams

Once there was a room full of cats. Cats were everywhere—on chairs, tables, even hanging from lamps. A mama mouse and her three babies went across the floor. All the cats got quiet and formed a line behind the mice. Then, all of a sudden, the mama mouse turned around and said, "BOW-WOW!" And all the cats ran away. Then the mama mouse turned to her babies and said, "It pays to know another language."

Grady Allen Smith

What did the gorilla use to fix the sink?
A monkey wrench.

Erik DiNardo

What do rabbits have that no other animals have?
Baby rabbits.

Leah Kubczak

Why don't chickens make good baseball players?
Because they can only hit fowl balls.

Wendy Fry

Why don't leopards play hide and seek?
Because they are always spotted.

Craig Bernotus

How do you keep a skunk from smelling?
Hold its nose.

Brandon Bulthuis

Who does a horse like best?
Its neigh-bors.

Allison Rogde

Why do monkeys scratch themselves?
Because they're the only ones who know where it itches.

Maria Aguirre

Why do mother kangaroos hate rainy days?
Because then their children have to play inside.

Tricia Lynn Payne

Why do cows give milk?
Because they aren't smart enough to sell it.

Jennifer Warmouth

What did the gorilla say when his sister had a baby?
"Well, I'll be a monkey's uncle."

Billy Garrett

Why did the chicken lay an egg?
Because if she dropped it, it would break.

Rusty Miller

How do you stop a bull from charging?
You take away its credit card.

Wendy Bryson

Why do birds fly south for the winter?
Because it's too far to walk.

Rachelle Farries

How do you catch a squirrel?
Climb up a tree and act like a nut.

Sandy Acreman

Why couldn't the pony sing?
Because it was a little hoarse.

Nathan Morales

Why should you never ask a Brontosaurus to tell you a bedtime story?
Because their tales are very long.

Ronald Darby

Where does a two-ton gorilla sit at the movies?
Wherever it wants.

Bryan Hoy

What is the first thing baby apes learn in school?
The Ape, B, C's.

Jill Kerby

Where do horses go when they are sick?
To the horspital.

Sarah Breeyear

What kind of pig likes to drive a car?
A road hog.

Anthony Loeffler

Elephant Express

Why do ducks have flat feet?
To stamp out forest fires.
Why do elephants have flat feet?
To stamp out burning ducks.

Lukas Plank

Who does an elephant call when its toe hurts?
A tow truck.

Alison Reese

Why did the elephant sit on the marshmallow?
To keep from falling in the hot chocolate.

Taj Gibbs

How do you make an elephant float?
Mix soda, syrup, ice cream and an elephant.

Suzanne Pagliorola

Why do elephants have trunks?
Because they would look silly carrying suitcases.

Tina Rose

What did the grape do when the elephant sat on it?
It let out a little whine.

Tatum Ward

How do you know if an elephant used your toothbrush?
It will smell like peanuts.

Mikelle Fretz

If an elephant didn't have a trunk, how would he smell?
Trunk or no trunk, he'd still smell terrible.

Christine Palkovic

Why can't two elephants go swimming at the same time?
Because they only have one pair of trunks.

Jennifer Chambers

What time is it when five elephants run after one elephant?
Five after one.

Amanda Moore

Icky & Ooky

Why did the fly fly?
Because the spider spied her.
Anne Shindel

What do you call spiders that get married?
Newlywebs.
Carrie Rentler

Do snakes need silverware when they eat?
No, because they have forked tongues.
Christi Dodd

What is a mosquito's favorite sport?
Skin diving.
Jaymi Bradford

Why was the insect kicked out of the forest?
Because it was a litterbug.
Elizabeth Burns

Why are snakes considered to be thrifty?
Because they can make both ends meet.
Kelly Coughlin

Why do spiders spin webs?
Because they don't know how to knit.
Erin Eickenhorst

Why do spiders make good baseball players?
Because they know how to catch flies.
Chris Pagleno

How does a bee comb its hair?
With a honey comb.
Cassie Lynne Peterson

What did the mama firefly say to the papa firefly?
"Isn't Junior bright for his age?"
Julie Schroeder

What is the first thing a snake learns in school?
Hisss-tory.
Elizabeth Noe

Ridiculous Riddles

When is a car not a car?
When it turns into a driveway.

Michael Johnson

Why was six afraid of seven?
Because seven, *ate,* nine.

Marci Healy

What is black and white and read all over?
A newspaper.

Tanya Mason

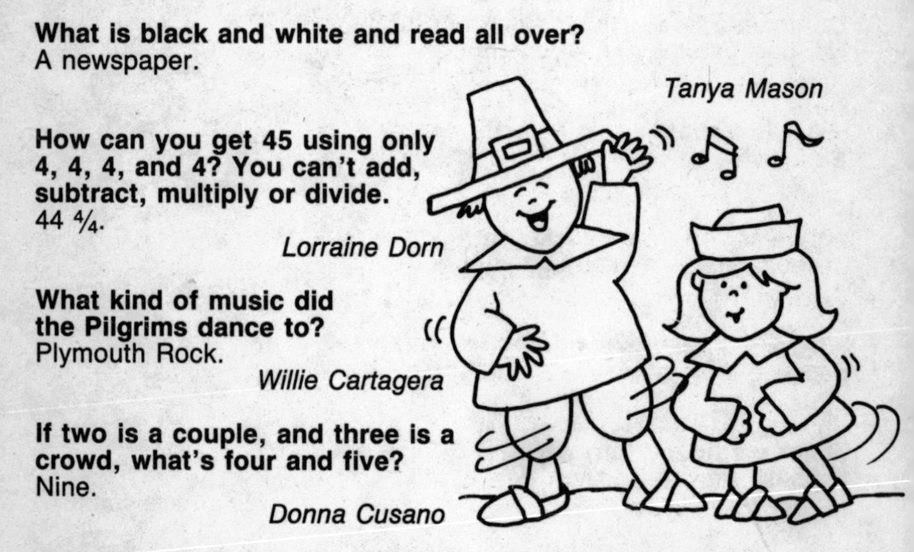

How can you get 45 using only 4, 4, 4, and 4? You can't add, subtract, multiply or divide.
44 4/4.

Lorraine Dorn

What kind of music did the Pilgrims dance to?
Plymouth Rock.

Willie Cartagera

If two is a couple, and three is a crowd, what's four and five?
Nine.

Donna Cusano

If it took 20 minutes for one man to fill a bathtub with water using one bucket, how long will it take for two men with two buckets to fill the same bathtub?
No time at all because the other man already filled it up.

Christie Cardarella

What time is it when the clock strikes thirteen?
Time to get a new clock.

Jason Chaney

What runs but never moves, and has hands but can't hold anything?
A clock.

Nathan Baird

What is fog?
A cloud that is afraid of heights.

Heather Donn Morgan

As long as I eat I am fine. But when I drink, I die. What am I?
A fire.

Candice Vinson

What starts with T, ends with T, and is full of T?
A teapot.

Brandi Jones

What has feet and legs, but cannot walk?
A pair of stockings.

Crystal Dawn Akers

What has a head and a tail but no body?
A coin.

Kandi Hankins

Why is the nose in the middle of the face?
Because it's the scenter.

Benjamin Florez

What has one foot at each end and has a third foot in the middle?
A yardstick.

Ashley Muratori

Why do dragons sleep all day?
Because they like to hunt knights.

Jon Barnes

How many seconds are in a year?
Twelve. There's January 2nd, February 2nd, March 2nd, April 2nd, May 2nd, June 2nd, July 2nd, August 2nd, September 2nd, October 2nd, November 2nd, and December 2nd.

Tara Holland

Someone takes this and you don't know what it looks like. You have never seen it before, but when you get it back you know it is yours. What is it?
Your picture.

Marisa McRainey

What are the two strongest days of the week?
Saturday and Sunday. The rest are weak days.

Amy Kay Hudson

Kooky Knock-Knocks

Knock! Knock!
Who's there?
Osborne.
Osborne who?
Osborne in Texas, how about you?

Nathaniel Hart-Benham

Knock! Knock!
Who's there?
Eliza.
Eliza who?
Eliza lot, so don't believe him.

Jerry Alexander

Knock! Knock!
Who's there?
Heaven.
Heaven who?
Heaven you heard this before?

Jessica Abler

Knock! Knock!
Who's there?
Scold.
Scold who?
S'cold outside, let me in.

Brian Poindexter

Knock! Knock!
Who's there?
Catsup.
Catsup who?
Cats up a tree.

Josh Lindsey

Knock! Knock!
Who's there?
Whenna.
Whenna who?
Whenna you gonna let me in?

Elizabeth Naylor

Knock! Knock!
Who's there?
Zoom.
Zoom who?
Zoom do you expect?
Heather Jordan

Knock! Knock!
Who's there?
Amos.
Amos who?
Amosquito bit me.
Knock! Knock!
Who's there?
Andy.
Andy who?
Andy bit me again.

Sarah Dowst

Knock! Knock!
Who's there?
Canoe.
Canoe who?
Canoe come out and play with me?

Nicole Condon

Vampires & Skeletons

Why do vampires play cards at the cemetery?
Because they can always dig up an extra player.

Gregory Van Dyke

Why did the little vampires stay up all night?
Because they were studying for a blood test.

Jeff McMurray

What's a vampire's favorite fruit?
A neck-tarine.

Erich Zorn

What test did Dracula take before the movie?
A scream test.

Marc Vasher

Where does Dracula work?
At the blood bank.

Ami Tulin

What is Dracula's favorite dog?
A bloodhound.

Jennifer Bellizzi

What is Dracula's favorite flavor of ice cream?
Vein-illa.

Steven Cundiff

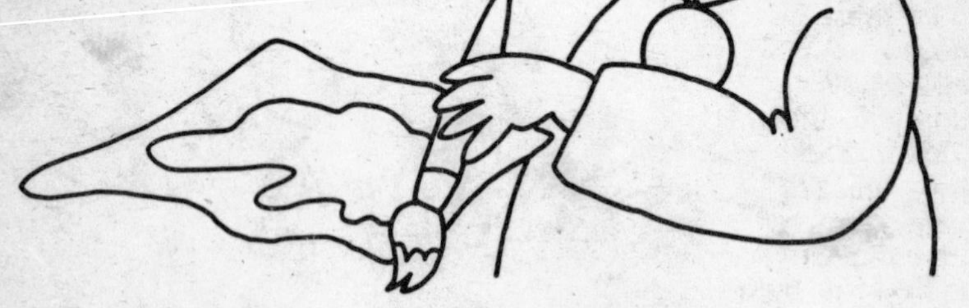

What did the vampire do at the art contest?
He drew blood.

Michael Bell

How many vampires does it take to change a light bulb?
None. Vampires prefer the dark.

Katy Decker

What does one angry skeleton say to another skeleton?
"I've got a bone to pick with you."

Albert Manuel

Why didn't the skeleton go to the ball?
Because he didn't have any body to go with.

Jeremy Christensen

Why don't vampires like sleeping people?
Because they don't like tired blood.

Charles Jones

Why did the skeleton go to the library?
Because he wanted to bone up on a few things.

Jason Higgerson

Why did the skeleton get such a high score on the quiz?
Because it got the bone-us question.

Kerriann Engholm

Why do vampires drink blood?
Because root beer makes them burp.

Kelly Nelson

Why do skeletons hate winter?
Because the cold goes right through them.

Heather Patrick

Why don't people like vampires?
Because they're a pain in the neck.

Mike Gonzales

What's as sharp as a vampire's fang?
His other fang.

Marlys Fassett

Who won the skeleton beauty contest?
Nobody.

Tammi Sramek

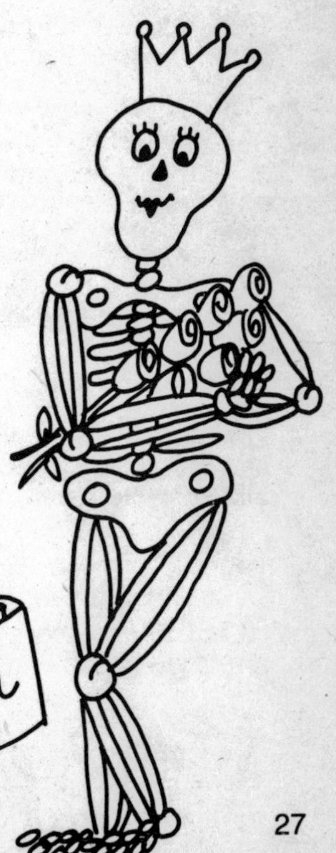

Odds & Ends

Where does the Lone Ranger take his trash?
To the dump, to the dump, to the dump, dump, dump.

David Dean

Why did the boy throw the letter out the window?
Because he wanted to send it air mail.

Chad Palmer

Why did the boy stand behind the donkey?
Because he thought he would get a kick out of it.

Ben Angley

What is the difference between a cat and a comma?
One has claws at the end of its paws, and the other has a pause at the end of its clause.

Jason Lee

Ted: Call your dog off.
Karen: I can't. I've called him Muffin ever since he was a pup.

Katrina Smolinski

One day, a boy walked into a fish store and said, "Throw your four biggest fish into the air—fast!" When the manager asked why, the boy said, "So I can honestly tell my mom I caught them."

Erin Harris

What should you do before you get off a bus?
Let it stop.

Jay Shipley

Jill: What is the first letter in yellow?
Terry: Y.
Jill: Because I want to know.

Jill Schultz

Jennifer: Did you know it takes three sheep to make a sweater?
Dawn: I didn't even know sheep could knit.

Joelle Proulx

Kim: Have you ever seen a barn dance?
Tim: No, but I've seen a chimney sweep.

Meghan Hicks

John: I don't understand it. If your father bought your mother a mink, why is she so mad?
Jeff: Because she has to clean out its cage.

John Hill

Bobby: I know someone who thinks he's an owl.
Danny: Who?
Bobby: Now I know two.

Jason Saniano

First Passenger: Do these buses run on time?
Second Passenger: No, they run on wheels.

Robert Young

How many months have 28 days in them?
All of them!

Melissa Musgrove

A man had two sons and named them both Ed. Why?
Because two Eds are better than one.

Nick Pakula

There were three men on an island. One man found a genie bottle. The genie said that he would grant them three wishes. The first man wished to be home with his family, and then he was. The second man wished for the same, and he too was gone. The third man felt kind of lonely, and said, "I wish my two friends were back."

Angela Barkley

Why did the boy put his father in the freezer?
So he would get a "pop"cicle.

Michelle Blocker

Jamie: Did your watch stop when it dropped on the floor?
Wesley: Of course it did. Did you expect it to go right through?

Jamie Knotts

Ghastly Ghouls

Why don't ghosts like rain?
Because it dampens their spirits.

Jarrod Canepa

What happened when the girl ghost met the boy ghost?
It was love at first fright.

Viviana Alonz

Why did the ghost like disco dancing?
Because it liked to boogie.

Kelly Davis

How can you tell if a mummy has been in your refrigerator?
The leftovers will be re-wrapped in bandages.

Charles Brinck

What is the most important rule for witches?
Don't fly off the handle!

Katie Peterman

What did the mother ghost say to the junior ghost in the car?
"Fasten your sheet belt."

Erin Hunter

What's worse than a witch without a broom?
A vampire with false teeth.

Eric Person

What did one ghost say to the other ghost?
"Do you believe in people?"

Krishanna Mask

What did the witch ask for in the hotel?
Broom service.

Krista Dorsaneo

Where do ghosts like to swim?
In the Dead Sea.

Lorenzo Graham

How can you make a witch scratch?
Take away the w and she'll itch.
Cybrian Williams

Where do spirits mail their letters?
At the ghost office.
Nicole Fuller

What is a witch's favorite subject?
Spelling.
Edward Avallone

What did the mother ghost tell her little ghost?
"Don't spook until you are spooken to."
Kris Robertson

What kind of witch rides a golden broom?
A rich witch.
Tammy Burgess

What does a ghost like to eat for lunch?
Booberry pie and I scream.
Allison David

When do ghosts play baseball?
When their spirit is catching.
Kate Whiting

Why did the little ghost flunk his spelling test?
Because he made too many boo-boo's.
Danielle Carson

Why does a witch fly on a broom?
So she won't be left in the dust.
Mary Kelly Carter

Why did the mummy skip lunch?
Because it was too wrapped up in its work.
David Theriault

...No Place Like Home

Young Man: Sir, I've come to ask for your daughter's hand in marriage.
Father: You'll have to take all of her or it's no deal.

Gopal Sachdeva

What is the last thing you take off when you go to bed?
You take your feet off the floor.

Kristen Hutson

Brother: I'm going to give Mom a beautiful cut-glass flower vase for her birthday.
Sister: But she already has a beautiful cut-glass flower vase.
Brother: No, she doesn't. I just dropped it.

Brooke Jackman

Why did the little boy take his bike to bed with him?
So he would not have to walk in his sleep.

Shannon Oliver

A mother and father were worried about their 5-year-old son. He never spoke a word in his life. One day at the breakfast table, the boy said, "Can I have some sugar on my cereal?" The mother and father were shocked and excited. The mother said to the boy, "Son, you can speak! Why haven't you ever said anything up till now?" The boy shrugged, and said, "Up till now, everything has been okay."

Marta deCandia

Why did the boy close his eyes when he looked in the mirror?
Because he wanted to see what he looked like when he was sleeping.

Stephanie Hall

(Suzie's teacher knocked on the door to her house.)
Teacher: Suzie, is your mother here?
Suzie: Nope, she ain't.
Teacher: Suzie, your grammar!
Suzie: She ain't here either.

Kim Humphries

Why did the boy disconnect his doorbell?
Because he wanted to win the "No-bell" Prize.

Sandi Krenz

Farm-Fresh Funnies

City Visitor: Look at that bunch of cows.
Farmer: Herd.
City Visitor: Heard of what?
Farmer: Herd of cows.
City Visitor: Sure! I've heard of cows.

Justin Stark

What did the cherry tree say to the farmer?
"Stop picking on me."

Dareece Williams

When is a chicken most likely to go into the hen house?
When the door is open.

Sonja Daniels

What did the cow ask the silo?
"Is my fodder in there?"

Mark Matson

Why do baby pigs eat so much?
Because they want to make hogs of themselves.

Naomi Caudle

Why did the farmer go over the potato crop with such a heavy roller?
Because he wanted to grow mashed potatoes.

Nathan Peterson

Why was the farmer so famous?
Because he was out standing in his field.

Joann Metz

Why don't farmers tell secrets on the farm?
Because the corn has ears, the potatoes have eyes, and the beans talk.

Lori Dubach

What should you do if a chicken lays a golden egg?
Tell it to lay more.

Kaiesha Flucas

What did the chick say to the other chick when the hen laid an orange instead of an egg?
"Look at the orange marmalade."

Joshua White

Down by the Sea

What did the girl octopus say to the boy octopus?
"I want to hold your hand, hand, hand, hand, hand, hand, hand, hand."

Lindsey Fillman

How do you correspond with a fish?
Drop it a line.

Sara Collett

Where do fish keep their money?
In the river bank.

Erica Neri

How does an octopus go into battle?
Well-armed.

Lisa Williams

Why are fish so smart?
Because they swim in schools.

Misty Jones

Where does a fish sleep?
In a water bed.

Chris Courchesne

What should you feed your pet frog?
Croakers and milk.

Timothy Cook

Why don't sea gulls ever fly across the bay?
Because then they would be bagels.

Jessica Mazella

What does a frog order at a snack bar?
French flies and a large croak.

Stephanie Munsterman

When does a duck wake up?
At the quack of dawn.

Allison Rudig

Why are baby tadpoles the best storytellers?
Because older frogs have lost their tales.

Katie Hillman

Off to Work We Go

Why did the man get fired from the orange juice factory?
Because he couldn't concentrate.

Amy Tolliver

How does an auctioneer look when conducting a sale?
For-bidding.

George Remus

What is the most useless invention?
A solar-powered flashlight.

David Ure

Why did the man wear boxing gloves on the freeway?
To fight the traffic.

Shaila Nevarez

When are cooks mean?
When they beat the eggs and whip the cream.

James Kearns

If a king sits on gold, who sits on silver?
The Lone Ranger.

Rachel Kitzman

Why does a candlemaker have it easy?
Because he only works on wick ends.

Derek Brown

What's the worst season of the year for a tightrope walker?
The fall.

Renee Southward

Why did the audience throw eggs at the actor?
Because ham and eggs go well together.

Cindy Crans

What does a baseball player do when he gets hot?
He stands in front of the fans.

Christy Tincher

Snicker Doodles

What part does a lion have in a play?
The mane part.

Kelly O'Connor

What time is it after dinner?
Ate o'clock.

Sarah Holmboe

If an airplane crashed on the border of the United States and Canada, where would you bury the survivors?
Nowhere. You don't bury survivors.

Daniel Hale

From what number can you take away half, and get nothing?
8. Take away the top half and you have 0.

Colleen Flanigan

If it's raining cats and dogs, what might you step in?
A poodle.

Daniel Dezinski

How can you double your money?
Put it in front of a mirror.

Corey Williams

What can you sit on, sleep on, and brush your teeth with?
A chair, a bed, and a toothbrush.

Meghan Holston

What kind of table has no legs?
A multiplication table.

Leigh Dunnam

How can you tell if a volcano is mad?
It will blow its top.

Jamie Parker

When does water stop running downhill?
When it gets to the bottom, of course!

Scott Helmbrecht

What was the longest line at the joker's party?
The punch line.

Erin Costanzo

What is the hottest day of the week?
Friday.

Beth Williams

What's easy to get into, but hard to get out of?
Trouble.

Jeffrey Carter

Why would most dogs make good archaeologists?
Because they like digging up old bones.

Joey Libby

Can two three-month-old dogs fall for each other?
Sure! But it'll only be puppy love.

Sabrina Rojas

What did the dog in the Old West say when it limped into town?
"I'm lookin' for the varmint who shot my paw."

Beth Ann Sinclair

Sue: What is your dog's name?
Dan: Ginger.
Sue: Does Ginger bite?
Dan: No, Ginger snaps.

Jennifer Brierley

Passenger: Is this my train?
Conductor: No, sir. It belongs to the railroad company.

Sara Smith

There once was a lady who married four men—a banker, an actor, a hairdresser, and an undertaker. One day a man asked why she married four men. She said, "One for the money, two for the show, three to get ready, and four to go."

Jody Fleury

P.U.!

What did the judge say when the skunk sprayed the court?
"Odor in the court."

Laura Houde

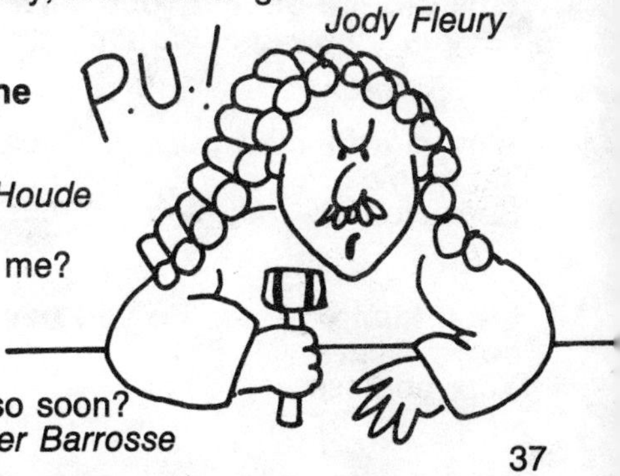

Mary: Will you always remember me?
Lou: Always.
Mary: Knock! Knock!
Lou: Who's there?
Mary: How could you forget me so soon?

Christopher Barrosse

Neighborhood Nonsense

Why did the girl sit on her watch?
Because she wanted to be on time.

Corinne Rios

If the red house is on the south side of the street, and the blue house is on the north side of the street, where is the White House?
In Washington, D.C.

Christina Butler

What's worse than raining cats and dogs?
Hailing taxis.

Angela Huff

What can go up the chimney down, but cannot go down the chimney up?
An umbrella.

Aaron Borling

How do leaves change in the fall?
Autumn-atically.

Jennifer Nahrebeski

Why do tea kettles whistle?
Because they never learned to sing.

Thomas Fraser

Why do traffic signals turn red?
You would too if you had to change in public.

Dina Sireika

Why did the old lady put roller skates on her rocking chair?
Because she wanted to rock and roll.

Heather Franck

Why did the man put the clock under his pillow?
Because he wanted to sleep over time.

Misty Brown

What kind of dress do you have, but never wear?
Your address.

Jennifer Goric

Charlie Buckner is a butcher. He has 20/20 vision, hears real well, and is very smart. What does he weigh?
Meat.

Elisa Ramos

What is the tallest building in New York City?
The library, because it has the most stories.

Nate Stulman

Ron: Where are you going with that watering can?
Don: To water the flowers.
Ron: But it's raining outside.
Don: That's okay, I have my raincoat on.

Cody Pitts

Tim: Did you hear about the big fight on the train last night?
Bill: No, what happened.
Tim: The conductor punched a ticket.

Jenny Scott

John and Mike had a table stuck in the doorway. After about 20 minutes, John said, "This table sure is hard to get in." "Get in?" asked Mike. "I've been pushing it out."

Debbie Jo Dolansky

Why did Jennifer go out with her purse open?
Because she was expecting some change in the weather.

Ryan P. Dunn

Boy: You should keep your eyes open tomorrow.
Girl: Why?
Boy: Because if you don't, you might bump into something.

Laura Mico-Monaco

Susan: Do you have holes in your socks?
Jennifer: No.
Susan: Then how do you get your feet in?

Jessica Mary Selander

Bill: This match won't light.
Jim: What's the matter with it?
Bill: I don't know. It worked great a minute ago!

Shawn Schnell

Customer: I would like these nails, please.
Clerk: That will be 59 cents plus tax.
Customer: I don't want tacks, just nails.

Kelley Dooley

Fun! Fun! Funny!

Teacher: Bobby, you were late for school this morning, you were late yesterday, and you were late the day before that. What is the matter?
Bobby: I can't help it. I run down Main Street every day. Then I come to a sign that says "SCHOOL - GO SLOW." So I do!

Elizabeth Smith

If one boy has 9 piles of hay, and another has 21 piles of hay, how many piles of hay do they have altogether?
One.

James Svesnik

If all the letters of the alphabet were invited to a tea party, what letters would be late?
The letters U, V, W, X, Y and Z, because they all come after T.

Lori Harms

What has 6 legs, 4 ears, 4 eyes, 1 tail, 2 mouths, and 2 noses?
A man riding a horse.

Raymond A.C. White

What part of a fish weighs the most?
The scales.

Tina Pappas

Mother: What did you learn in school today?
Daughter: Not enough. I have to go back tomorrow.

Tammie Davis

Why did the man put bandages on his refrigerator?
Because it had cold cuts.

Lisa Huddleston

What makes more noise than one squealing pig?
Two squealing pigs.

Gail McKinney

What kind of truck do farmers take their pigs to market in?
In a pig up truck.

Natalie Gillespie

Barb: Which hand do you stir your cocoa with?
Ben: Neither, I use a spoon.

Brandy Broussard

Why did the boy stand on his head?
Because he was trying to turn things over in his mind.

Quincy D. Edison

What has four wheels and flies?
A garbage truck.

Rachel Gibbs

A Special Thanks To:

Abler, Jessica, 8, Sacred Heart School, Norfolk, NE
Acreman, Sandy, 10, Dunbar Elem., Ramer, AL
Aguirre, Maria, 8, L.K. Hall Elem., Dallas, TX
Akers, Crystal Dawn, Grade 4, Booker T. Washington School, Lexington, KY
Alexander, Jerry, 11, York School, Springfield, MO
Alonz, Viviana, 8, St. Anselm School, Bronx, NY
Angley, Ben, 7, Flint River Academy, Woodbury, GA
Arbour, Tommy, 11, Our Lady of Mercy School, Baton Rouge, LA
Arrigo, Andrea, 10, St. Clare School, Staten Island, NY
Avallone, Edward, 8, Saint Stephen School, Hamden, CT
Bainter, Raquelle, 10, Hoxie Grade School, Hoxie, KS
Baird, Nathan, Grade 1, Indianapolis Public School No. 61, Indianapolis, IN
Baldwin, Emily, 8, P.S. 87 Manhattan, New York, NY
Barb, Jeremy, 11, Triplett Middle, Mount Jackson, VA
Barkley, Angela, 10, Clover Middle, Clover, SC
Barnes, Jon, 7, Lincolnview East Elem., Middle Point, OH
Barrosse, Christopher, 8, Our Lady Star of the Sea School, New Orleans, LA
Beier, Carmen, 12, Our Savior Lutheran School, Fenton, MO
Bell, Michael, 8, Hagerstown Elem., Hagerstown, IN
Bellizzi, Jennifer, 8, Eli Whitney School, Stratford, CT
Bernotus, Craig, 8, Timothy Ball Elem., Crown Point, IN
Bledsoe, Rebecca, 9, Fair Grove School, Thomasville, NC
Blocker, Michelle, 11, Holland Hall School, Tulsa, OK
Boemi, Nicole, 10, St. Clare School, Staten Island, NY
Bonarigo, David, 11, Liberty School, Orland Park, IL
Borling, Aaron, 11, Liberty School, Orland Park, IL
Bowen, Christine, 9, Balboa Street Magnet School, Northridge, CA
Bradford, Jaymi, 9, Fair Grove School, Thomasville, NC
Breeyear, Sarah, 8, Grand Isle Elem., Grand Isle, VT
Brierley, Jennifer, 7, Lonsdale Elem., Lincoln, RI
Brinck, Charles, 9, Paulding Elem., Paulding, OH
Broussard, Brandy, 11, Our Lady of Mercy School, Baton Rouge, LA
Brown, Chris, 6, Carolyn Wenz School, Paris, IL
Brown, Derek, 10, Tinicum Elem., Pipersville, PA
Brown, Misty, 10, MGM School, Farrell, PA

Bryson, Wendy, Grade 2, Wetumpka Elem., Wetumpka, AL
Bullock, April Bree, 11, Collins Middle, Collins, MS
Bulthuis, Brandon, 7, Wheatfield Elem., Wheatfield, IN
Burgess, Tammy, 9, Wernert Elem., Toledo, OH
Burns, Elizabeth, 9, Pinecrest School, Greenwood, SC
Butala, Mike, 8, Bartman Elem., Hermitage, PA
Butler, Christina, 5, Carolyn Wenz School, Paris, IL
Callan, Katie, 8, Carlisle Elem., Carlisle, IA
Campanaro, Jenny, 8, Spring Garden Elem., Bedford, TX
Campbell, Tara, 8, Manchester Elem., Manchester, KY
Canepa, Jarrod, 10, St. Clare School, Staten Island, NY
Cardarella, Christie, 10, Henry Barnard School, Enfield, CT
Caris, Stacie, 10, W.H. Rhodes Elem., Milton, FL
Carson, Danielle, 7, Fairview Elem., Mora, MN
Cartagera, Willie, 9, Joel School, Clinton, CT
Carter, Jeffrey, 7, Lincoln Park Elem., Knoxville, TN
Carter, Mary Kelly, 9, Seven Oaks Elem., Columbia, SC
Caudle, Naomi, 10, W.H. Rhodes Elem., Milton, FL
Chambers, Jennifer, 7, Piedmont Elem., Dandridge, TN
Chandiramani, Rachna, 10, Gateway Upper Elem., Monroeville, PA
Chaney, Jason, 8, Hagerstown Elem., Hagerstown, IN
Charles, Andrea, 7, Ramon C. Cobbs Lower, Newark, DE
Christensen, Jeremy, 9, Johnson Elem., Mesa, AZ
Church, Amanda, Grade 3, Central Elem., Clinton, IN
Ciregna, Steven, 9, St. Athanasius School, Brooklyn, NY
Collett, Sara, 6, Coral Springs Elem., Coral Springs, FL
Condon, Nicole, 8, Highlands Elem., Wilmington, DE
Connors, Cheryl, 10, St. Benedict Joseph Labre School, Richmond Hill, NY
Cook, Timothy, 11, Houston Middle, Houston, MS
Costanzo, Erin, 11, St. Odilia School, Shoreview, MN
Coughlin, Kelly, 8, Orange Avenue School, Cranford, NJ
Courchesne, Chris, 7, Veterans Park School, Ludlow, MA
Crans, Cindy, 11, Our Lady of Mount Carmel School, Boonton, NJ
Cumberland, Amanda, 8, Ricardo Elem., Kingsville, TX
Cunat, Jimmy, 9, Liberty School, Orland Park, IL
Cundiff, Steven, 10, Lincoln School, Bedford, IN
Cusano, Donna, 8, Saint Stephen School, Hamden, CT
Dagostino, Lucilla, 10, Hampton School, Hampton, NJ
Daniels, Sonja, 9, 60th Street School, Niagara Falls, NY
Darby, Ronald, 9, Manchester School, Windham, ME
Dattilio, Erica, 7, Paramount School, Hagerstown, MD
David, Allison, 9, Norton Elem., Snellville, GA
Davis, Kelly, 11, Littleton Elem., Cashion, AZ
Davis, Tammie, 9, Gandy Elem., White Hall, AR
Day, Eric, 8, Highlands Elem., Wilmington, DE
Dean, David, 11, Demarest Elem., Demarest, GA
deCandia, Marta, 8, Robert L. Craig School, Moonachie, NJ
Decker, Katy, Grade 4, Our Lady Of Lourdes, Hitchcock, TX
DeLaire, Nichole, 8, Our Lady Czestochowa School, Coventry, RI
DeLano, Stephanie, 10, Kramer Middle, Willimantic, CT
Denlinger, Tommie, 8, Paradise Elem., Paradise, PA
Dezinski, Daniel, 9, Crescentwood School, East Detroit, MI

DiNardo, Erik, 6, Cedar Hill School, Towaco, NJ
Dodd, Christi, 9, Howe Valley School, Cecilia, KY
Dolansky, Debbie Jo, 8, St. Elizabeth Elem., Pittsburgh, PA
Dooley, Kelley, 11, St. Odilia School, Shoreview, MN
Dorn, Lorraine, 9, Southwood Elem., Old Bridge, NJ
Dorsaneo, Krista, 10, St. Callistus School, Philadelphia, PA
Dowst, Sarah, 10, Old County Road School, Esmond, RI
Dubach, Lori, 11, Geneva Elem., Geneva, IN
Dunn, Ryan P., 11, Our Lady of Mount Carmel School, Boonton, NJ
Dunnam, Leigh, 8, St. Pius X School, Mobile, AL
Edison, Quincy D., Grade 4, Booker T. Washington School, Lexington, KY
Eickenhorst, Erin, 7, Nathan Hale School, Manchester, CT
Enderby, Matt, 6, Lincolnview East Elem., Middle Point, OH
Engholm, Kerriann, 10, St. Odilia School, Shoreview, MN
Esposito, Lauren, 7, Alburtis School, Alburtis, PA
Evanush, Nikki, 9, Bonny Kate School, Knoxville, TN
Falkner, Haddi, 7, Bartman Elem., Hermitage, PA
Farries, Rachelle, 9, Hueytown Elem., Hueytown, AL
Fassett, Marlys, 9, Morgan School, Beloit, WI
Feulner, Jason, 8, Severn School, Corning, NY
Fike, Joy, 9, Bradford Elem., Bradford, OH
Fillman, Lindsey, 8, Ramon C. Cobbs Lower, Newark, DE
Flanigan, Colleen, 10, St. Michael School, Livonia, MI
Fleury, Jody, 8, Brewerton Elem., Brewerton, NY
Florez, Benjamin, 7, Noble Elem., Cleveland Heights, OH
Flucas, Kaiesha, 9, L.L. Hotchkiss Montessori Academy, Dallas, TX
Fraerman, Andrew, 6, South School, Glenco, IL
Franck, Heather, 9, St. Johns Lutheran School, Napa, CA
Fraser, Thomas, 9, St. Clare School, Staten Island, NY
Frederickson, Penny, 8, Wakefield Elem., Wakefield, NE
Fretz, Mikelle, 7, Liberty School, Scottsdale, AZ
Friese, Laura, 10, Flanagan Jr. High, Flanagan, IL
Frohnheiser, Lisa, 10, St. Anne School, Bethlehem, PA
Fry, Wendy, 7, Wheatfield Elem., Wheatfield, IN
Fuller, Nicole, 8, Westside Elem., Daytona Beach, FL
Furnival, Jodi, 8, Park School, Munhall, PA
Galati, Vanessa, 8, Deer Park Avenue Elem., North Babylon, NY
Gallagher, Jessicah, 7, McNair School, Hazelwood, MO
Garrett, Billy, 10, Lynn Kirk Elem., Youngstown, OH
Garrison, Cindy, 10, Opdyke Grade School, Opdyke, IL
Gibbs, Rachel, 10, Peavine School, Reno, NV
Gibbs, Taj, Grade 3, Pine Lake Elem., Miami, FL
Gillespie, Natalie, 10, Tazewell Elem., Tazewell, VA
Gobel, April, 7, Andover Elem., Andover, KS
Gonzales, Mike, 9, Mitchell Elem., Racine, WI
Goric, Jennifer, 8, Windmere School, Ellington, CT
Graham, Lorenzo, 10, MGM School, Farrell, PA
Greening, Erin, 9, Liberty School, Orland Park, IL
Hale, Daniel, 10, St. Michael School, Livonia, MI
Hall, Denece, 9, Palm Vista Elem., 29 Palms, CA
Hall, Stephanie, 11, Bondurant Middle, Frankfort, KY
Hallowell, Jesse, 10, Tinicum Elem., Pipersville, PA

Hankins, Kandi, 7, Ajo Elem., Ajo, AZ
Harms, Lori, 10, Flanagan Jr. High, Flanagan, IL
Harris, Erin, 11, Blackburn Elem., Independence, MO
Harris, Marquist, 9, Jimmy Brown Elem., Star City, AR
Harrison, Liam E., 9, Gayhead Elem., Hopewell Junction, NY
Hart-Benham, Nathaniel, 10, John F. Long Elem., Phoenix, AZ
Healy, Marci, 11, Blessed Trinity School, Ocala, FL
Heineke, Amy, 9, Morgan School, Beloit, WI
Helmbrecht, Scott, 8, Fairview Elem., Mora, MN
Hicks, Meghan, 10, St. Odilia School, Shoreview, MN
Higgerson, Jason, 8, McNair School, Hazelwood, MO
Hill, John, 8, Newport Elem., Newport, NC
Hillman, Katie, 8, Lenox School, Portland, OR
Hines, Robert, Grade 2, University Lab School, Baton Rouge, LA
Holland, Tara, 9, Augusta Christian School, Martinez, GA
Holmboe, Sarah, 8, Orchard Hills School, Novi, MI
Holston, Meghan, 9, St. Pius X School, Mobile, AL
Horvath, Ryan, 8, Liberty School, Scottsdale, AZ
Houde, Laura, 8, Towpath School, Avon, CT
Hoy, Bryan, 7, Prides Corner School, Westbrook, ME
Huddleston, Lisa, 9, Gandy Elem., White Hall, AR
Hudson, Amy Kay, 11, Doyle-Ryder School, Flint, MI
Huff, Angela, 11, Oak Grove West School, Bartonville, IL
Humphries, Kim, 11, Bluestem Middle, Leon, KS
Hunter, Cindy, 10, McKinley School, Huron, SD
Hunter, Erin, 8, Orchard Hill Farm School, Tinley Park, IL
Hushagen, Danny, 7, Fairview Elem., Mora, MN
Hutson, Kristen, 9, North Elem., Marshall, IL
Jackman, Brooke, 10, Vernon Middle, East Norwich, NY
Johnson, Michael, 9, St. Andrew School, Orlando, FL
Johnston, Megan, 7, Park School, Munhall, PA
Jones, Brandi, 11, Meadowview Elem., Bossier City, LA
Jones, Charles, 10, Beck Elem., Columbus, OH
Jones, Derron, Grade 4, Booker T. Washington School, Lexington, KY
Jones, Misty, 9, Hueytown Elem., Hueytown, AL
Jordan, Heather, 6, Prides Corner School, Westbrook, ME
Kearns, James, 8, Liberty School, Scottsdale, AZ
Kendrick, Jonathan, Grade 2, University Lab School, Baton Rouge, LA
Kerby, Jill, 8, Spencer Elem., Spencer, WV
Kitzman, Rachel, 9, Converse School, Beloit, WI
Knotts, Jamie, 10, Flemington Elem., Flemington, WV
Kobolt, Holly, 11, Eastgate Middle, Kansas City, MO
Krenz, Sandi, 10, St. Odilia School, Shoreview, MN
Kubczak, Leah, 7, Erskine School, Cedar Rapids, IA
Lantz, Megan, 9, Pine Butte Elem., Colstrip, MT
Lee, Jason, 9, Augusta Christian School, Martinez, GA
Lee, Travis, 10, Walnut School, Chino, CA
Libby, Joey, 10, 60th Street School, Niagara Falls, NY
Lieb, Brenda, 7, Penns Manor Elem., Clymer, PA
Lindsey, Josh, 8, Fouke Elem., Fouke, AR
Link, Theresa, 8, St. Francis Xavier School, Cresson, PA
Lloyd, Sarah, 10, Wimbledon Courtenay School, Wimbledon, ND
Loeffler, Anthony, 9, Carl Sandburg Elem., Littleton, CO

Madonna, Allison, 7, Villa Maria Academy Lower, Immaculata, PA
Malaythong, David, Grade 1, Nevada Community School, Nevada, IA
Mangabang, Aaron, 11, Mary Immaculate School, Farmers Branch, TX
Manuel, Albert, 7, Ajo Elem., Ajo, AZ
Mask, Krishanna, 7, Howe Avenue School, Sacramento, CA
Mason, Tanya, 10, W.H. Rhodes Elem., Milton, FL
Matson, Mark, Grade 2, Vineland Elem., Rotunda West, FL
Mazella, Jessica, 10, St. Clare School, Staten Island, NY
McAuliffe, Kristen, 9, Kingston Elem., Kingston, MA
McCleary, Charley, 8, Windmere School, Ellington, CT
McClendon, Matt, 7, South Euless Elem., Euless, TX
McCracken, Erin, 7, Stoneleigh Elem., Baltimore, MD
McCulken, Christine, 10, St. Callistus School, Philadelphia, PA
McGovern, Kristy, 9, St. Thela School, Chicago, IL
McKinney, Gail, Grade 5, Morgantown Elem., Morgantown, KY
McMurray, Jeff, 9, Palm Vista Elem., 29 Palms, CA
McRainey, Marisa, 9, King Springs Elem., Smyrna, GA
Mertz, Jennifer, 9, Richland Elem., Quakertown, PA
Metz, Joann, 8, Crothersville Elem., Crothersville, IN
Mico-Monaco, Laura, 9, Van Sciver School, Haddonfield, NJ
Miller, Rusty, 8, Flint River Academy, Woodbury, GA
Minster, Sara, 9, Walnut School, Chino, CA
Molesky, Joseph, 9, Cherry Elem., Iron, MN
Molinares, Jessica, 10, St. Benedict Joseph Labre School, Richmond Hill, NY
Moore, Amanda, 7, R. Elisabeth Maclary Primary, Newark, DE
Moore, Conor, 7, Nathan Hale School, Manchester, CT
Morales, Nathan, 9, Foley Elem., Foley, AL
Morgan, Heather Donn, 8, Jefferson Elem., Jefferson, TX
Moser, Anna, 10, South Jordan Elem., South Jordan, UT
Moyer, Donald, 7, R. Elisabeth Maclary Primary, Newark, DE
Munsterman, Stephanie, 7, Southeast School, Clinton, MO
Muratori, Ashley, 8, St. Mary School, Sandusky, OH
Murphy, Patrick, 8, Tualatin Elem., Tualatin, OR
Musgrove, Melissa, 9, Gandy Elem., White Hall, AR
Muskie, Dan, 11, St. Francis of Assisi School, Springfield, PA
Nahrebeski, Jennifer, 11, McKinley Intermediate, Lackawanna, NY
Naylor, Elizabeth, 8, Hayward Elem., Hayward, WI
Nelson, Kelly, 8, Cherry Elem., Iron, MN
Neri, Erica, 7, A.H. Rockwell School, Bethel, CT
Nevarez, Shaila, 8, Waggoner School, Winters, CA
Nieken, Danny, 8, Wheatfield Elem., Wheatfield, IN
Noe, Elizabeth, 10, Gandy Elem., White Hall, AR
Norman, Tonetta, 11, P.S. 103, Bronx, NY
O'Connor, Kelly, 9, Liberty School, Orland Park, IL
Oliver, Shannon, 7, Camden Elem., Camden, NY
Pagleno, Chris, 10, Reid Elem., Athens, AL
Pagliorola, Suzanne, 5, River Plaza School, Red Bank, NJ
Pakula, Nick, 7, Corpus Christi School, Milwaukee, WI
Palkovic, Christine, 9, Lynn Kirk Elem., Youngstown, OH
Palmer, Chad, 8, Falling Creek Elem., Elberton, GA
Pappas, Tina, 9, Roosevelt School, Peru, IL
Parker, Jamie, 9, Andover Elem., Andover, KS
Patrick, Heather, 6, Wallace Elem., Bristol, VA

Payne, Tricia Lynn, 8, J.F. Gauthier Elem., St. Bernard, LA
Pecson, Lorena S., 10, Washington Elem., Hawthorne, CA
Person, Eric, 9, Liberty School, Orland Park, IL
Peterman, Katie, 8, Elsie C. Johnson School, Hanover Park, IL
Peterson, Cassie Lynne, Grade 2, E.N. Nordgaard Elem., Glenwood, MN
Peterson, Nathan, 8, Carlisle Elem., Carlisle, IA
Pitts, Cody, 9, Bauer-Speck School, Paso Robles, CA
Plank, Lukas, 9, Lake Placid Elem., Lake Placid, NY
Plata, Rocio, 8, L.K. Hall Elem., Dallas, TX
Podobinski, AnnMarie, 11, St. Odilia School, Shoreview, MN
Poindexter, Brian, 9, Jimmy Brown Elem., Star City, AR
Powers, Gary, 9, Tygart School, Parkersburg, WV
Proulx, Joelle, 8, Charlton Street School, Southbridge, MA
Pruitt, Brian, 11, O.P. Earle Elem., Landrum, SC
Puffer, Thomas Richard, 6, Hitchcock Elem., Hitchcock, SD
Ramos, Elisa, 11, Meadowview Elem., Bossier City, LA
Reding, David, 10, Palm Vista Elem., 29 Palms, CA
Reese, Alison, 9, Martin Luther King, Jr. Elem., Wilmington, DE
Remus, George, 8, St. John of the Cross School, Western Springs, IL
Rentler, Carrie, 7, Nathan Hale School, Manchester, CT
Rios, Corinne, 10, Busansky School, Pemberton, NJ
Rivenburg, Stacey, 9, Maine Memorial School, Maine, NY
Rivera, Michael, 11, Public School #4, Cliffside Park, NJ
Robertson, Kris, 10, Higgins Intermediate, Whitehouse, TX
Rogde, Allison, 8, Raguet Elem., Nacogdoches, TX
Rojas, Sabrina, 10, Bobby Duke Middle, Coachella, CA
Rose, Tina, 10, Sycamore School, Kokomo, IN
Rudig, Allison, 8, Tualatin Elem., Tualatin, OR
Russell, Marlena, 9, Fremont Older School, Cupertino, CA
Sachdeva, Gopal, 10, St. Benedict Joseph Labre School, Richmond Hill, NY
Sadowski, Tabitha, 8, Bartman Elem., Hermitage, PA
Saniano, Jason, 9, Western Branch Elem., Chesapeake, VA
Santoli, Anthony, 7, School No. 10, Belleville, NJ
Santone, Nicholas, 9, St. Callistus School, Philadelphia, PA
Scheffy, Rebecca, Grade 2, University Lab School, Baton Rouge, LA
Schmelzer, Jessica, 10, Clyde Erwin Elem., Jacksonville, NC
Schnell, Shawn, 9, Riveredge Elem., Berea, OH
Schroeder, Julie, 9, Wakefield Elem., Wakefield, NE
Schultz, Jill, 8, Minot Forest School, Wareham, MA
Scott, Jenny, 10, Grand Terrace Elem., Colton, CA
Selander, Jessica Mary, 9, Eli Whitney School, Stratford, CT
Sheehan, Joshua M., 9, John F. Long Elem., Phoenix, AZ
Shelton, Jason, 10, W.H. Rhodes Elem., Milton, FL
Shindel, Anne, 7, Hayshire Elem., York, PA
Shipley, Jay, 11, York School, Springfield, MO
Siewert, Shane, 9, Pine Butte Elem., Colstrip, MT
Sinclair, Beth Ann, 7, Glendale Elem., Flinton, PA
Sireika, Dina, 11, McKinley Intermediate, Lackawanna, NY
Sloan, Josh, 8, Carlisle Elem., Carlisle, IA
Smith, Elizabeth, 7, Lonsdale Elem., Lincoln, RI
Smith, Grady Allen, 11, Augusta Raa Middle, Tallahassee, FL
Smith, Sara, 11, Opdyke Grade School, Opdyke, IL
Smith, Thomas, 9, Fremont Older School, Cupertino, CA

Smolinski, Katrina, 10, Freeland Elem., Freeland, MI
Smythe, John, 11, Riccardi Elem., Glasco, NY
Southward, Renee, 9, Woodbury Elem., Woodbury, MN
Spitzer, Bradley, 7, Big Hollow School, Ingleside, IL
Sprouse, Jennifer, 8, Carlisle Elem., Carlisle, IA
Sramek, Tammi, Grade 5, Brooks School, Lewistown, MT
Stark, Justin, 8, Deer Park Avenue Elem., North Babylon, NY
Stewert, Kimberly, 6, Hilltop School, Caribou, ME
Stombres, Stefanie, 8, Kaneland Elem., Maple Park, IL
Strait, Taylor, 9, Seven Oaks Elem., Columbia, SC
Stulman, Nate, 9, Bigelow Hill School, Findlay, OH
Sunny, James, 10, Galena Middle, Galena, IL
Svesnik, James, Grade 4, West Hempfield Elem., Irwin, PA
Symonds, Andy, 9, Palm Vista Elem., 29 Palms, CA
Taylor, Angie, 7, Wickford Elem., North Kingstown, RI
Theriault, David, 7, Prides Corner School, Westbrook, ME
Tincher, Christy, 9, Custer School, Broken Bow, NE
Tindall, Matt, 7, Dawkins Middle, Spartanburg, SC
Tolliver, Amy, 5, Grove Elem., Montrose, IL
Tolman, Joleen, 8, Charlton Street School, Southbridge, MA
Tucci, Jennifer, 9, All Saints School, Pottsville, PA
Tulin, Ami, 10, Kramer Middle, Willimantic, CT
Twomey, Kevin, 10, St. Michael School, Livonia, MI
Tycer, Haley Dean, 9, Lewis Vincent Elem., Denham Springs, LA
Ure, David, 6, South School, Glenco, IL
van der Linde, Jason, 11, Our Savior Lutheran School, Fenton, MO
Van Dyke, Gregory, 8, T.R. Elem., Oyster Bay, NY
Vasher, Marc, 7, Vineland Elem., Rotunda West, FL
Vinson, Candice, 7, North Elem., Breckenridge, TX
Wang, Judy, 7, R. Elisabeth Maclary Primary, Newark, DE
Ward, Tatum, 11, Sycamore School, Kokomo, IN
Warmouth, Jennifer, 9, Lynn Kirk Elem., Youngstown, OH
Wasilchuk, Libby, 11, Vernon Middle, East Norwich, NY
White, Joshua, 9, Lexington Elem., Monroe, LA
White, Raymond A.C., 8, Saipan Community School, Saipan, MP
Whiting, Kate, 8, Lake Park School, Albany, GA
Williams, Beth, 7, Hopkins Elem., Richmond, VA
Williams, Corey, 8, Shades Mountain School, Birmingham, AL
Williams, Cybrian, 9, Opa Locka Elem., Opa Locka, FL
Williams, Dareece, 8, P.S. 250, Brooklyn, NY
Williams, Lisa, 11, Howe Valley School, Cecilia, KY
Williams, Matthew, 8, Log Pile School, Washington, PA
Wilson, Cindy, Grade 2, South Cumberland Elem., Crossville, TN
Winkel, Robert, 7, Judson School, Watertown, CT
Winston, Elisha, 10, C.G. Credle School, Oxford, NC
Wood, Kathryn, 10, St. Michael School, Livonia, MI
Wootton, Jason, 7, R. Elisabeth Maclary Primary, Newark, DE
Wright, Daniel, 9, P.J. Hill School, Trenton, NJ
Wyatt, Brandi, Grade 2, South Cumberland Elem., Crossville, TN
Young, Jonas, Grade 1, Indianapolis Public School No. 61,
Indianapolis, IN
Young, Robert, 9, Jimmy Brown Elem., Star City, AR
Zorn, Erich, 8, Bon Meade Elem., Coraopolis, PA